New**Start** Hymns and Songs

the official
Churches Together Collection
for the Millennium and beyond

First published in Great Britain in 1999 by
KEVIN MAYHEW LIMITED
Buxhall
Stowmarket
Suffolk IP14 3DJ

Compilation © Kevin Mayhew Ltd 1999

The right of Kevin Mayhew Ltd to be identified
as the compilers and editors of this work
has been asserted by them in accordance with the
Copyright, Designs and Patents Act 1988.

All rights reserved. No part of this publication may be reproduced,
stored in a retrieval system, or transmitted, in any form or
by any means, electronic, mechanical, photocopying,
recording or otherwise, without the prior
written permission of the publisher.

The words of most of the songs in this publication are covered by a
Church Copyright Licence which allows local church reproduction on
overhead projector acetates, in service bulletins, songsheets, audio/visual
recording and other formats. Full details of the licence are available from:

Christian Copyright Licensing Ltd., PO Box 1339
Eastbourne, East Sussex BN21 4YF

Telephone: 01323 417711   Fax: 01323 417722

The following editions are available

Words Only	ISBN	1 84003 326 6
	ISMN	M 57004 566 2
	Catalogue No.	1413101
Full Music	ISBN	1 84003 327 4
	ISMN	M 57004 522 8
	Catalogue No.	1413104

Cover design by Jaquetta Sergeant
Typesetting by Richard Weaver
Printed and bound in Great Britain

Foreword

The Christian Churches of England have never worked so closely together on any major celebration as they have done for the Millennium celebration. A huge range of Christians – Catholics, Anglican, Nonconformist, Black Churches, New Churches – have come together to promote a New Start in this nation.

A New Start is at the heart of the Gospel, and is the central message that the Churches have for the world as we enter the third Millennium.

So it is with very great pleasure that we commend to all of our Churches this supplement of new hymns and songs for worship. It deliberately draws from all the Christian traditions of worship represented in our Millennium celebrations. The editorial board was chosen to reflect all these traditions in their rich diversity, and has commissioned a collection which celebrates the New Start and the New Millennium. May this hymn book add to our understanding and our common worship as we enter the adventure of the third Millennium of our Lord.

Baroness Richardson
Bishop Crispian Hollis
Bishop Gavin Reid

Editorial Board

Mrs Wanda Adams
The Harmony Trust

Mr Malcolm Archer
Organist and Master of Choristers, Wells Cathedral

Mr Ken Burton
Principal Conductor, London Adventist Chorale
and Croydon SDA Gospel Choir

The Revd Brian Hoare
Former President of the Methodist Conference

Abbot Alan Rees, OSB
Choirmaster of the Monastic Community at
Belmont Abbey, Hereford

Canon Michael Saward
Canon of St Paul's Cathedral, London

The Revd Richard Thomas
Director of Communications, Oxford Diocese

The Revd Roger Whitehead
Secretary of the Churches' Group for Evangelisation

Introduction

At the heart of the Christian Gospel is the call to inclusiveness. No one is outside the embracing love of God who goes to the Cross for each one of us, and as Christ himself prayed for unity, we are called as Churches to model this inclusiveness.

So when a new collection of songs and hymns for the Millennium was proposed by the Churches' Millennium Group, it was clear that it had to reflect this inclusiveness. All Christian traditions would be invited to contribute, and the collection would be the first ever produced that was deliberately intended to reflect all these traditions.

The Millennium message of the Churches is simply the offer of a New Start – a New Start for the world's poor, a New Start at home, and a New Start with God. The Thematic Index is divided into these three headings so that worship can be planned around this Millennium message.

Putting this collection together has been an exciting project. The editorial board met only twice, and did much of its work at a distance. I am grateful to my colleagues for their help and advice, and to Kevin Mayhew and Jonathan Bugden for their gentle and patient guidance.

We offer this collection in a spirit of prayer, that it may enrich the worship of the Christian Churches at the start of a new Millennium of hope and inclusiveness.

The Revd Richard Thomas
Chairman, Editorial Board

The Millennium Resolution

Let there be
    respect for the earth
    peace for its people
    love in our lives
    delight in the good
    forgiveness for past wrongs
    and from now on a new start

1 *Christopher Ellis*

1. Almighty God, we come to make confession,
   for we have sinned in thought and word and deed.
   We now repent in honesty and sorrow;
   forgive us, Lord, and meet us in our need.

2. Forgiving God, I come to make confession
   of all the harm and hurt that I have done;
   of bitter words and many selfish actions,
   forgive me, Lord, and make me like your Son.

3. Forgiving God, I come to make confession
   of all that I have failed to do this day;
   of help withheld, concern and love restricted,
   forgive me, Lord, and lead me in your way.

4. Redeeming God, we come to seek forgiveness,
   for Jesus Christ has died to set us free.
   Forgive the past and fill us with your Spirit
   that we may live to serve you joyfully.

© *1999 Kevin Mayhew Ltd*

2 *Christopher Ellis*

1. At the heart of all things
   there is love, as Christ has shown.
   God of love, we praise you:
   healing, binding, making one.

2. Pulsing through creation,
   life of God and life for all:
   love is invitation,
   human future, God's own call.

3. Love is kind and patient,
   never boastful, never rude;
   love can cope with all things,
   overcoming selfish mood.

4. Trusting, hoping, loving:
   Jesus shows us how to care;
   love is still the best way,
   sign of life for all to share.

© *1999 Kevin Mayhew Ltd*

3 *Brian Hoare*

1. Beyond the fringes of the church,
   but not beyond the love of God,
   a restless world about its work
   seeks meaning deeper than it knows:
   communities whose common life
   ignores so much that Jesus taught.
   It was for them, not us alone,
   that Jesus came and lived and died and rose.

   To them we go
   your love to share;
   Good News for all
   ev'rywhere!
   Your kingdom comes,
   where Christ is Lord,
   and all the world
   obeys your word.

Continued overleaf

2. Beyond the fringes of the church,
   but not beyond the love of God,
   are thousands more who do not
     know
   the joy we celebrate today.
   Teach us to demonstrate your truth
   in ways their culture understands;
   and make us bold to speak of you,
   and point them all to Christ the
     Living Way.

   To them we go
   your love to share;
   Good News for all
   ev'rywhere!
   Your kingdom comes,
   where Christ is Lord,
   and all the world
   obeys your word.

   © Brian Hoare/Jubilate Hymns

4   *Marjorie Dobson*

1. Birth brings a promise of new life
     awaking,
   dawning of hope through a child's
     open eyes.
   Uncharted future is there for the
     making,
   challenge and change in a baby's
     first cries.

2. Ev'ry new life changes those who
     are round it
   making demands of commitment
     and care,
   calling for love to enfold and
     surround it,
   reshaping patterns by claiming a
     share.

3. Jesus, the new-born, crossed time's
     moving stages
   changing their course by the act of
     his birth,
   translating God from the myst'ry of
     ages,
   rooting our faith by his presence on
     earth.

4. Wonder and worship were waiting
     to greet him,
   love and devotion were his to
     command,
   life was transformed for the ones
     sent to meet him,
   touching their God in a child's
     outstretched hand.

5. Birth gives a promise of new life
     awaking.
   Jesus, the new-born, calls us to new
     birth.
   All that he promised is ours for the
     taking
   when our commitment brings God
     down to earth.

© Stainer & Bell Ltd

5   *Brian Hoare*

Blessing and honour, glory and power
are rightly yours, all-gracious God.
Blessing and honour, glory and power
are rightly yours, all-gracious God.

1. God, our creator,
   your mighty power
   has made all things
   to serve your will;
   you fill the heavens,
   earth shows your glory,
   and just and true
   are all your ways!

2. Jesus, our Saviour
   you left the heavens,
   and came to earth
   in human form;
   humbly obedient,
   you died to save us,
   but now you live
   as Lord of all!

3. O Holy Spirit,
   breath of the Father,
   poured out on all
   to make us new;
   life-giving Spirit,
   fountain of goodness,
   you fill your church
   with love and power!

© *Brian Hoare/Jubilate Hymns*

6 *John Aspinwall*

1. Bright, bright, the shining of
      Christ's saving way.
   Ever new, the timeless Easter day,
   whose life-giving light searches
      deep, makes all things whole.
   Jesus, fill us with your radiant soul.

2. Deep, deep the anguish of this
      broken world.
   Torn with sorrow streams our joy
      unfurled –
   a joy in the beauty of this so fragile
      earth.
   Jesus, life affirm; inspire new birth.

3. Brave, brave the voices that
      protesting cry –
   cry for justice and humanity.
   Cast out on the edge, on the
      margin, life denied,
   Jesus, show to us your wounded side.

4. Far, far the galaxies extend their
      scope.
   Vast our wonder, yet profound our
      hope.
   Our world has evolved through
      unfathomable grace.
   Jesus, bond in peace this sacred
      place.

5. Call, call us onward, let the scene
      unfold.
   Time's deep fountain flows to form
      and mould.
   Your word is our rock; holy wisdom
      is our guide.
   Jesus, be our star amid the tide.

6. Change, change is all around; the
      prospect new.
   Grace transforming re-creates the
      view.
   The old order fades; fresh
      perspectives greet the sight.
   Jesus, ever be our Way, our Light.

© *1999 Kevin Mayhew Ltd*

7 *Basil E. Bridge*

1. But when the time had fully come,
   the time by God appointed,
   when all the past would be fulfilled,
   there came among us, as God
      willed,
   the Christ, the Lord's anointed.

2. But when the time had fully come
   how few had recognised him!
   They never dreamt God's Son could
      be
   that carpenter from Galilee;
   their lack of faith surprised him.

Continued overleaf

3. But when the time had fully come
his close companions failed him;
then, handed over by a friend,
both church and state conspired his end;
upon a cross they nailed him.

4. But when the time had fully come
not evil's worst endeavour
could hold him in the tomb; the hour
of hope fulfilled had dawned; the power
of love holds good for ever.

© 1999 Kevin Mayhew Ltd

8 *Brian Hoare*

Celebrate the faith together:
Jesus Christ is King for ever!
Ev'ry voice in ev'ry place
sing to the Lord for his love and his grace.
Come from ev'ry church tradition,
one in faith and one in mission.
Share the news with ev'ryone,
tell ev'rybody that Jesus the Saviour has come.

1. We believe Christ is Lord,
Son of God, Living Word,
crucified, ris'n again,
this is the gospel that we proclaim!

2. What we know we declare:
news to tell, Christ to share.
Spread the Word, name the Name:
this is the gospel that we proclaim.

© Brian Hoare/Jubilate Hymns

9 *Martin E. Leckebusch*

1. Christ brings the kingdom where barrenness blooms:
see how the image of God is restored,
yielding a harvest of talents and skills
when we acknowledge our Maker as Lord.

2. Come to his kingdom of weakness made strong,
brokenness mended, the blind given sight;
welcome and dignity crown the despised,
darkness is banished by glorious light.

3. Come to his kingdom where righteousness reigns –
God has commanded: repent and believe!
Children of dust in his glory may share,
penitent rebels his favour receive.

4. Come to his kingdom of laughter and hope,
savour the freedom its fullness will bring:
no more oppression, injustice or fear –
come to the kingdom where Jesus is King!

© 1999 Kevin Mayhew Ltd

10 *Marjorie Dobson*

1. Christian people, sing together,
   all united in one voice.
   Though we come from many
      cultures,
   yet in Christ we all rejoice.
   In our daily lives we're scattered,
   serving God in various ways.
   Then in worship we're united,
   giving him our thanks and praise.

2. God created countless faces,
   yet in Christ we all are one.
   Though we look from many angles,
   all our views reflect the Son.
   So we bring each gift and talent,
   off'ring what we have to share,
   and God blends us all together
   in one body of his care.

3. Teach us, Lord, to trust each other,
   though our ways are not the same.
   As you call us to your purpose,
   bless our working in your name.
   In the world of daily living
   each uniquely serves your will,
   show how ev'ry person matters,
   as our calling we fulfil.

© 1999 Kevin Mayhew Ltd

11 *Michael Forster*

1. Come and join the great uprising,
      life begins again,
   springing up triumphant out of
      tragedy and pain,
   death has been defeated and its idol
      shall not reign,
   this is the world's new beginning.

   *Rejoice! Rejoice! The captives are
      released.
   Rejoice! Rejoice! Death's reign of fear
      has ceased.
   Evil is defeated by the Prince of love
      and peace,
   this is the world's new beginning.*

2. Jesus has defeated all manipulative
      powers,
   proven the futility of fortresses and
      towers;
   victims of oppression share the
      triumph of this hour:
   this is the world's new beginning.

3. Life in all its fullness is his gift for
      us to share:
   wholeness and security for people
      everywhere.
   Dare we live his life, to make
      creation just and fair?
   This is the world's new beginning.

4. Share the resurrection hope and put
      an end to fear,
   sorrow turns to joy and life eternal
      starts right here!
   Heav'n and earth unite to give a
      great resounding cheer!
   This is the world's new beginning.

© 1999 Kevin Mayhew Ltd

12 *Martin E. Leckebusch*

1. Come, wounded Healer, your
      sufferings reveal –
   the scars you accepted, our anguish
      to heal.
   Your wounds bring such comfort in
      body and soul
   to all who bear torment and yearn
      to be whole.

Continued overleaf

2. Come, hated Lover, and gather us near,
your welcome, your teaching, your challenge to hear:
where scorn and abuse cause rejection and pain,
your loving acceptance makes hope live again!

3. Come, broken Victor, condemned to a cross –
how great are the treasures we gain from your loss!
Your willing agreement to share in our strife
transforms our despair into fullness of life.

© 1999 Kevin Mayhew Ltd

13 *Jan Berry*

1. Creating God, we bring our song of praise
for life and work that celebrate your ways:
the skill of hands, our living with the earth,
the joy that comes from knowing our own worth.

2. Forgiving God, we bring our cries of pain
for all that shames us in our search for gain:
the hidden wounds, the angry scars of strife,
the emptiness that saps and weakens life.

3. Redeeming God, we bring our trust in you,
our fragile hope that all may be made new:
our dreams of truth, of wealth that all may share,
of work and service rooted deep in prayer.

4. Renewing God, we offer what shall be
a world that lives and works in harmony:
when peace and justice, once so long denied,
restore to all their dignity and pride.

© 1999 Kevin Mayhew Ltd

14 *Chris Bowater and Ian Taylor*

1. Creation is awaiting the return of the King.
The trees are poised to clap their hands for joy.
The mountains stand majestic to salute their God;
the desert lies in wait to burst into bloom.

The King is coming,
the King is coming,
the King is coming
  to set creation free.
(Repeat)

2. The church is awaiting the return of the King.
The people joined together in his love.
Redeemed by his blood,
washed in his word.
As a bride longs for her bridegroom,
the Church looks to God.

The King is coming,
the King is coming,
the King is coming
  to receive his bride.
(Repeat)

3. The world is awaiting the return of
    the King.
  The earth is a footstool for his feet.
  Every knee will bow down,
  every tongue confess,
  that Jesus Christ is Lord
  of heaven and earth.

The King is coming,
the King is coming,
the King is coming
  to reign in majesty.
(Repeat)

© 1999 Sovereign Lifestyle Music

15 *Mike Anderson*

Dance in your Spirit,
we dance in your Spirit,
we dance in your Spirit of joy!

1. Jesus, you showed us the way to
    live,
  and your Spirit sets us free,
  free now to sing, free to dance and
    shout,
  'Glory, glory' to your name.

2. Jesus, you opened your arms for us,
  but we nailed them to the cross;
  but you are risen and now we live,
  free from, free from ev'ry fear.

3. Your Spirit brings peace and
    gentleness,
  kindness, self-control and love,
  patience and goodness and faith
    and joy,
  Spirit, Spirit fill us now.

© 1999 Kevin Mayhew Ltd

16 *Catherine Williams*

1. Deep within the shadow of your
    wings
  I will rest,
  I will stay.
  Ready as the eagle to arise
  I will wait in you,
  O my Lord.

2. Growing in the vineyard of your
    care
  I will rest,
  I will stay.
  Grafted as a branch upon the vine
  bearing fruit for you,
  O my Lord.

3. Hidden in the quiver of your love
  I will rest,
  I will stay.
  Ready as your arrow to be sent
  to a waiting world,
  O my Lord.

© Catherine Williams

17 *John L. Bell and Graham Maule*

1. Ev'ry fiftieth year
  set the captives free:
  let a trumpet blast,
  summon jubilee.

Continued overleaf

And God bless the people,
the poor, tired and torn;
for it's in their lives
that love must be reborn.

2. Let the earth find rest
   where no rest is known:
   give the world's oppressed
   what should be their own.

3. Cancel every debt,
   terminate all fraud;
   let the use of wealth
   serve the cause of God.

4. Let the hills resound,
   let the oceans roar,
   celebrate the good,
   heaven and earth restore.

And God bless the people,
the poor, tired and torn;
for it's in their lives
that love must be reborn, reborn.

© Copyright WGRG, Iona Community/Wild Goose Publications

18 Graham Kendrick

1. First light is upon our faces,
   first light of the morning sun,
   first sight of a new creation,
   first hour of the age to come.

2. New life from the earth is waking,
   first shoots of the second birth,
   first bloom of an endless springtime,
   first bud of the tree of life.

3. First rays of the sun of justice,
   first note of the freedom song,
   first breath of the coming Spirit,
   first shout from the conquered tomb.

4. First light is the Father's glory,
   first light is the risen one,
   first born over all creation,
   we greet the unconquered Son.

5. First sound of a sacred rhythm,
   first beat of a different drum,
   first step of a dance with heaven,
   first joy of the world to come.

6. Last sigh of an age that's passing,
   last chill of a winter's breath,
   last night of the king of terrors,
   last days of the sting of death.

7. First light is the Father's glory,
   first light is the risen Son,
   the first and the last of all things,
   Jesus the Light has come!

© *1999 Ascent Music*

19 Michael Forster

God made a boomerang and called it love,
God made a boomerang and called it love,
God made a boomerang and called it love,
and then he threw it away!

1. Love's like a boomerang, that's what we've found,
   it comes right back when you throw it around.
   Something we can share out
   never seems to wear out,
   love's like a boomerang, let's throw it around.

2. Love's like a boomerang, that's what
      God planned,
   but it's no use if it stays in your hand.
   Gotta send it spinning
   for a new beginning,
   love's like a boomerang, let's throw
      it around.

3. Love's like a boomerang, goes with
      a swing,
   now ev'rybody can have a good fling.
   Families and nations
   join the celebrations,
   love's like a boomerang, let's throw
      it around.

© 1999 Kevin Mayhew Ltd

20 *Christopher Idle*

1. God of all human history,
   of time long fled and faded,
   yours is the secret mastery
   by which the years are guided:
   King of unchanging glory
   from ages unrecorded.

2. God of the hidden future
   unfolding life for ever,
   hope of each ransomed creature
   as time speeds ever faster:
   raise us to our full stature
   in Christ, our one Redeemer.

3. God of this present moment
   requiring our decision,
   now is the hour of judgement
   for ruin or salvation:
   give us complete commitment
   to your most urgent mission.

© Christopher Idle/Jubilate Hymns

21 *Elizabeth Cosnett*

1. God of every changing season,
   inner worlds and outer space,
   still beyond the grasp of reason,
   yielding still to love's embrace,
   we, your people, make
      thanksgiving,
   bridging culture, language, race,
   for the faith that Christ is living,
   for two thousand years of grace.

2. When, in savage mock-
      enthronement,
   Jesus died on Calvary,
   then was made a real atonement,
   rooted deep in history.
   Partners now in new creation,
   sharing all its joy and pain,
   pierced with glad anticipation,
   we await his final reign.

3. God, as Holy Spirit working,
   help us meanwhile find and clear
   all the mines of hatred lurking
   in the no-man's-land of fear.
   Do not let us worship money,
   lost in deserts made by greed,
   while your land of milk and
      honey
   waits to satisfy our need.

4. In the world's ongoing story
   now a new page open lies.
   Print it, Lord, with grace and glory,
   read it with our Saviour's eyes.
   Through all trials keep before us
   symbols faith will recognise,
   cross and crown, to reassure us
   God, our source, is God, our prize.

© 1999 Kevin Mayhew Ltd

22 *Jean Holloway*

1. God of love, you freely give us
   blessings more than we deserve;
   Be our light in times of darkness,
   be our strength when fears unnerve.
   In this age when proof convinces,
   Help us see where wisdom lies;
   More enduring than persuasion
   is your truth which never dies.

2. Son incarnate, yours the presence
   which can heal an aching heart;
   Over death you reign triumphant,
   You alone new life impart.
   From your birth so long awaited,
   to the cross on Calvary,
   You will serve as our example,
   Let us, Lord, your servants be.

3. Holy Spirit, inspiration
   day by day, yet mystery;
   With the Son and the Creator
   You form mystic unity.
   Draw us into your communion,
   With the love that sets us free;
   Bind our hearts to you for ever,
   Holy, blessèd Trinity.

© *1999 Kevin Mayhew Ltd*

23 *Christopher Ellis*

1. God of mission, still you send us
   to a world that needs your grace.
   You have gone ahead to meet us,
   you are waiting in each place.
   Show us now your loving glory
   in each child of ev'ry race.

2. God of hope, you call your people
   to become the future now!
   Help us see your will more clearly,
   grant us visions, show us how
   in your strength, despite our weakness,
   we might live your kingdom now.

3. You have called us to be partners
   in the mission of your Son.
   Black and white and male and female,
   you have called us to be one.
   Teach us how to serve together
   that through us your will be done.

© *1999 Kevin Mayhew Ltd*

24 *Peter Trow*

1. God of the passing centuries,
   of time completed and to come:
   we bring our prayer that you will make
   our longing and our living one.

2. Give us the wisdom, purpose, strength,
   to cherish all your hand has made,
   that ev'ry nation, ev'ry child,
   may live in peace, be unafraid.

3. We seek, for living fuller lives,
   with stranger, neighbour, loved one, friend,
   the love which you intend for all,
   which finds in Christ its source and end.

4. To all that brings delight in life,
   moments of vision, joyful days,
   all that has shaped us: leads us on,
   we say our 'Yes' with thanks and praise.

5. God of forgiveness set us free
   from suffered and inflicted pain,
   heal us from hatred born of fear,
   empower us all for life again.

6. That with the turning of the year,
   renewed in hope and glad of heart,
   safe in the knowledge of your grace,
   we may from now, make a new start.

© 1999 Kevin Mayhew Ltd

25 *Timothy Dudley-Smith*

1. God whose love is ev'rywhere
   made our earth and all things fair,
   ever keeps them in his care,
   praise the God of love!
   He who hung the stars in space
   holds the spinning world in place;
   praise the God of love!

2. Come with thankful songs to sing
   of the gifts the seasons bring,
   summer, winter, autumn, spring;
   praise the God of love!
   He who gave us breath and birth
   gives us all the fruitful earth;
   praise the God of love!

3. Mark what love the Lord displayed,
   all our sins upon him laid,
   by his blood our ransom paid;
   praise the God of love!
   Circled by that scarlet band
   all the world is in his hand;
   praise the God of love!

4. See the sign of love appear,
   flame of glory, bright and clear,
   light for all the world is here;
   praise the God of love!
   Gloom and darkness, get you gone!
   Christ the Light of life has shone;
   praise the God of love!

© Timothy Dudley-Smith

26 *Basil Bridge*

1. Gracious God, in adoration
   saints with joy before you fall;
   only when our hearts are leaden
   can we fail to hear their call:
   'Come with wonder, serve with gladness
   God whose power created all.'

2. Earth and sky in silent praises
   speak to those with eyes to see;
   all earth's living creatures echo
   'God has made us!' So may we
   come with wonder, serve with gladness
   him through whom they came to be.

3. You have made us in your image,
   breathed your Spirit, given us birth;
   Jesus calls, whose cross has given
   ev'ry life eternal worth,
   'Come with wonder, serve with gladness,
   let God's will be done on earth!'

4. Earth by war and want is threatened;
   deep the roots of fear and greed;
   let your mercy be our measure
   as we see our neighbour's need,
   come with wonder, serve with gladness,
   share your gift of daily bread.

Continued overleaf

5. Holy Spirit, urging, striving,
   give us love that casts out fear,
   courage, seeking peace with justice,
   faith to make this message clear –
   'Come with wonder, serve with gladness,
   live in hope; the Lord is near!'

© 1999 Kevin Mayhew Ltd

27 *Christopher Walker*

Great is the power we proclaim now,
as we worship and praise God's name.
For the glory of God is revealed as we pray:
Come, Lord, come, Lord, and live in us today.

1. God's people called to serve
   as disciples of the Lord.
   Gifts of the Spirit
   for us to inherit,
   to build up the Body of Christ.

2. God's people called to bring
   to the world the peace of Christ.
   Love for our neighbour,
   and justice in our labour,
   compelled by the love of Christ.

3. God's people called to pray
   for the Church to be made one.
   One holy nation
   in hope of salvation,
   brothers and sisters in Christ.

4. God's people called today
   to make known the love of God.
   Seeds we are sowing
   with faith that is growing
   strong in the power of Christ.

5. God's people called to share
   in the blessing cup of Christ:
   bread that is broken,
   and Word that is spoken,
   one in the Body of Christ.

© 1999 Christopher Walker

28 *Timothy Dudley-Smith*

1. Here on the threshold of a new beginning,
   by grace forgiven, now we leave behind
   our long-repented selfishness and sinning,
   and all our blessings call again to mind:
   Christ to redeem us, ransom and restore us,
   the love that holds us in a Saviour's care,
   faith strong to welcome all that lies before us,
   our unknown future, knowing God is there.

2. May we, your children, feel with Christ's compassion
   an earth disordered, hungry and in pain;
   then, at your calling, find the will to fashion
   new ways where freedom, truth and justice reign;
   where wars are ended, ancient wrongs are righted,
   and nations value human life and worth;
   where in the darkness lamps of hope are lighted
   and Christ is honoured over all the earth.

29
Geoff Baker

1. If my people who are called by my name
will humble themselves and pray;
if my people will seek my face
and turn from their wicked ways,
then I will hear from heaven and forgive them.
Then I will hear from heav'n and heal their land.
My eyes are open and my ears are listening.
Come, my people, hear and understand.

2. We, your people, who are called by your name,
will humble ourselves and pray.
We, your people, will seek your face,
and turn from our wicked ways.
O Father, hear from heaven and forgive us.
O Father, hear from heav'n and heal our land.
Your eyes are open and your ears are listening
as your people hear and understand.

© 1999 Sovereign Music UK

3. So may your wisdom shine from scripture's pages
to mould and make us stones with which to build
God's holy temple, through eternal ages,
one church united, strong and Spirit-filled;
heirs to the fullness of your new creation
in faith we follow, pledged to be your own;
yours is the future, ours the celebration,
for Christ is risen! God is on the throne!

© Timothy Dudley-Smith

30
Nick Fawcett

1. I hear somebody calling, a voice from far away;
it's crying out for justice, and yearning for that day
when no one need go hungry, despair will be no more –
a day which gladly heralds a new start for the poor.

2. I hear somebody calling, a voice from somewhere near;
it's crying out with longing, yet no one seems to hear.
Despite long years of witness, a multitude still search –
forgive us, Lord, and grant now a new start for the church.

3. I hear somebody calling, a voice from all around;
it's crying out in anguish, the grim and tragic sound
of God's creation groaning, stripped bare, denied her worth –
Lord, curb our greed, and bring now a new start for the earth.

Continued overleaf

4. I hear somebody calling, a voice
      from close at hand;
   it's crying out in anger,
      campaigning for a land
   where all will be respected, and war
      will find no place –
   a world of peace and friendship, a
      new start for our race.

5. I hear somebody calling, a voice
      from deep within;
   it's crying out for mercy, confessing
      all my sin.
   Lord come to me, I beg you, for I
      have lost my way –
   reach out in love and grant now a
      new start for today.

6. I hear somebody calling, a voice
      from far above;
   it's crying out in sorrow, and urging
      us to love,
   for still a world lies bleeding, the
      weak go to the wall –
   God grant in your great mercy a
      new start for us all.

© 1999 Kevin Mayhew Ltd

2. We have built discrimination
      on our prejudice and fear;
   hatred swiftly turns to cruelty
      if we hold resentments dear.
   For communities divided
      by the walls of class and race
   hear our cry and heal our nation:
      show us, Lord, your love and grace.

3. When our families are broken;
      when our homes are full of strife;
   when our children are bewildered,
      when they lose their way in life;
   when we fail to give the aged
      all the care we know we should –
   hear our cry and heal our nation
      with your tender fatherhood.

4. We who hear your word so often
      choose so rarely to obey;
   turn us from our wilful blindness,
      give us truth to light our way.
   In the power of your Spirit
      come to cleanse us, make us new:
   hear our cry and heal our nation
      till our nation honours you.

© 1999 Kevin Mayhew Ltd

31 *Martin E. Leckebusch*

1. In an age of twisted values
      we have lost the truth we need;
   in sophisticated language
      we have justified our greed;
   by our struggle for possessions
      we have robbed the poor and weak –
   hear our cry and heal our nation:
      your forgiveness, Lord, we seek.

32 *James Quinn*

1. In the silence of the Godhead
      there is born the Father's Word,
   God from God and light eternal,
      his belov'd and only Son;
   in their rapture of communion
      breathes the Spirit of their love,
   one God in Trinity.

2. Through his Word the gracious Father
   bids the world in splendour rise;
   man and woman in God's image
   bear the imprint of his love;
   to their care is now entrusted
   all the beauty of the earth,
   one world in harmony.

3. When they turn from their Creator
   God in mercy sends his Son;
   he will take our human nature
   to redeem the world from sin,
   to restore love's broken image
   in the hearts that love has made,
   in love that knows no end.

4. In the silence of Good Friday
   all the world in darkness lies,
   for the light of all the ages
   in the sleep of death is found;
   but the seed of God's great harvest
   waits to rise at God's command,
   the living Word of God.

5. In the dawn of Easter Sunday
   death and sin are overcome;
   Christ, the Lord of life, is risen,
   glorious firstborn from the dead;
   in this springtime of creation
   Christ has made the world anew
   in love and unity.

6. Glory be to God the Father,
   fount from whom all blessings flow;
   glory be to God, our Saviour,
   King of kings and Lord of lords;
   glory be to God the Spirit,
   bond of love in unity,
   one God in Trinity.

© *Geoffrey Chapman, an imprint of Cassell plc*

33 *David Bartleet*

1. I saw the wind in the sky,
   the sparkle of fire in the dew,
   dance of a child in the sand,
   the steps of the old.
   Give me your eyes, living Lord,
   for loving today.

2. I felt the breeze in my hair,
   the warmth of the sun in my heart;
   I felt the presence of joy,
   the touch of a hand.
   Make me aware, living Lord,
   for loving today.

3. I heard the flight of the gulls,
   the boom of the sea in the caves,
   groaning of rocks in the earth,
   a cry from the heart.
   Give me your ears, living Lord,
   for loving today.

4. I know the pulse of my blood,
   the freshness of life in my breath,
   I sense the source of my soul,
   the well-spring divine.
   Give me your power, living Lord,
   for loving today.

5. I know the darkness of sin,
   the blight of my guilt and despair,
   I know the coming of love,
   the lifting of heart.
   Give me your grace, living Lord,
   for loving today.

6. I have a pathway to tread,
   a place at the table to fill;
   destiny shaped by your hands,
   a vision of joy.
   Give me yourself, living Lord,
   for loving today.

© *1999 David Bartleet*

34 *Margaret Rizza*

1. Jesus, in the new dawn, guide our way,
   lead us to your light;
   Jesus, in the new dawn, guide our way,
   free us from our strife;
   Jesus, in the new dawn, fill our world,
   bless us with your joy;
   Jesus, in the new dawn, fill our world,
   bring us to your truth.

2. Spirit, in the new dawn, sing to us,
   play for us your song;
   Spirit, in the new dawn, sing to us,
   we will join your dance;
   Spirit, in the new dawn, take our hearts,
   birth in us your peace;
   Spirit, in the new dawn, take our hearts,
   make them one with yours.

3. Father, in the new dawn, speak to us,
   plant in us your love;
   Father, in the new dawn, speak to us,
   teach us to forgive;
   Father, in the new dawn, hold us fast,
   bring us to new life;
   Father, in the new dawn, hold us fast,
   bind us to your heart.

© 1999 Kevin Mayhew Ltd

35 *Basil E. Bridge*

1. Jesus, in your life we see you
   making God's compassion known,
   'Surely you have borne our sorrows,
   surely made our pain your own!'
   see your touch bring hope and healing,
   see your word set captives free,
   see you suffer, mocked, rejected,
   dying on the shameful tree.

2. Risen Lord, you reign in glory;
   but your wounded hands still show
   you can share the outcast's torment,
   sound the depths of human woe,
   know where greed exploits the helpless,
   hear the addict's lonely cry,
   grieve at so much waste and heartbreak,
   feel for all who question 'why?'

3. Risen Lord, you bear their sorrow,
   know how much they need your peace;
   as you once healed broken bodies,
   offered captive souls release,
   take us, use us in your service;
   we would follow where you lead;
   only your divine compassion
   meets the depths of human need.

© 1999 Kevin Mayhew Ltd

36 *Nick Fawcett*

1. Jesus, the broken bread, we come to you;
   empty, we would be fed – meet us anew.
   Teach us to hunger after righteousness,
   reach out in love, we pray, to guide and bless.

2. Jesus, the poured out wine, we come with awe;
   thirsty, we take the cup – quench and restore.
   Teach us to seek your kingdom and your will,
   reach out in love, we pray, our lives to fill.

3. Jesus, the crucified, we come with shame;
   greedy, we've sought reward – made that our aim.
   Teach us to worship now through word and deed,
   reach out in love, we pray, to all in need.

4. Jesus, the risen Lord, we come with praise;
   gladly, we sing of you, our hearts ablaze.
   Teach us to glimpse new life beyond the grave,
   reach out in love, we pray, to heal and save.

5. Jesus, the living one, we come with joy,
   truly, no evil can your love destroy.
   Teach us to walk in faith, though hope seems vain,
   reach out in love, we pray, renew again.

6. Jesus, the King of kings, we come to serve,
   freely give all for you as you deserve.
   Teach us to share the love you daily show,
   reach out in love, we pray, and bid us go.

© 1999 Kevin Mayhew Ltd

37 *Michael Forster*

1. Join the glorious celebration,
   with the God of re-creation:
   every race and every nation,
   make a brand new start!
   Hear the people singing!
   Hear the gospel ringing:
   love for life,
   an end to strife,
   and truth eternal springing.
   That's the hope, though some despise it:
   God has pledged to realise it.
   Raise the song to advertise it:
   make a brand new start!

Continued overleaf

2. Round the world, the news is flying,
   where the hungry poor are dying,
   hear the voice of protest crying:
   'Make a brand new start!'
   God himself is calling,
   urgent and appalling!
   See his face,
   in ev'ry place,
   where tears of rage are falling:
   bring an end to exploitation,
   centuries of domination,
   break the chains that bind each nation:
   make a brand new start.

3. Praise the God who sought and found us
   when the chains of sin had bound us,
   spoke the words that still astound us:
   'Make a brand new start!'
   God of incarnation,
   be our inspiration;
   love be known
   and justice shown
   throughout your whole creation:
   earth and heav'n in Christ united,
   saints and sinners all invited,
   love resplendent, God delighted!
   Make a brand new start!

© 1999 Kevin Mayhew Ltd

38 *Rick Wakeman*

1. Just one world, just one world,
   full of sadness for our maker,
   who gave his Son, gave his life
   and died to save us all.

   *And if you see the way of life ahead,
   and free your hearts and lives of sin,
   then our world lives again,
   lives again in him.*

   *Father, Son and Holy Ghost,
   blessed Trinity.*

2. Just one word, holy word,
   here on earth, as our salvation,
   to help us live, live again,
   to live again through him.

© Copyright 1999 Tuesday Music (UK)

39 *Martin E. Leckebusch*

1. Let us rejoice: God's gift to us is peace!
   Here is the calm which bids our strivings cease,
   for God's acceptance brings a true release:
   alleluia!

2. We can be strong, for now we stand by grace,
   held in his loving, fatherly embrace;
   his care remains, whatever trials we face:
   alleluia!

3. We trust in God – and shall not be dismayed,
   nor find our hopes of glory are betrayed,
   for all his splendour we shall see displayed:
   alleluia!

4. And come what may, we never need
      despair –
   God is at work through all the
      griefs we bear,
   that in the end his likeness we may
      share:
   alleluia!

5. Deep in our hearts the love of God
      is found;
   his precious gifts of life and joy
      abound –
   so let our finest songs of praise
      resound:
   alleluia!

   © 1999 Kevin Mayhew Ltd

40 *David Mowbray*

1. Light a candle for thanksgiving!
   Sing to God for Christ the Lord!
   Born to Mary, dying, living;
   still the Spirit speaks his word.
   Welcome ev'ry tower pealing,
   celebrate two thousand years!
   Years of grace and years revealing
   Christ where Christlike love
      appears.

2. Light a candle for achievers!
   Marvel at their range of thought:
   artists, scientists, believers
   famed for what their hands have
      wrought.
   For the feats of engineering,
   for each fresh, creative probe;
   ev'ry benefit appearing,
   spread across a shrinking globe.

3. Light a candle for the nation
   and the future of its youth!
   Build with them on this
      foundation:
   love, security and truth.
   Christ the Lord, by patience
      winning
   many a household, many a heart,
   set ablaze their faith's beginning,
   journey with them from the start.

4. Light a candle for tomorrow!
   Ask that countries may walk free:
   truly free, not bound to borrow,
   but released for jubilee.
   One has come among us bearing
   news that prisoners are restored:
   let his voice move us to sharing –
   sing to God for Christ the Lord!

   © David Mowbray/Jubilate Hymns

41 *Jan Berry*

1. Living God, your word has called us,
   summoned us to live by grace,
   make us one in hope and vision,
   as we gather in this place.
   Take our searching, take our praising,
   take the silence of our prayer,
   offered up in joyful worship,
   springing from the love we share.

2. Living God, your love has called us
   in the name of Christ your Son,
   forming us to be his body,
   by your Spirit making one.
   Working, laughing, learning,
      growing,
   old and young and black and white,
   gifts and skills together sharing,
   in your service all unite.

   Continued overleaf

3. Living God, your hope has called us
   to the world that you have made,
   teaching us to live for others,
   humble, joyful, unafraid.
   Give us eyes to see your presence,
   joy in laughter, hope in pain.
   In our loving, in our living,
   give us strength that Christ may reign.

© 1999 Kevin Mayhew Ltd

4. Winter now has passed and gone:
   spring is here;
   climate's changed, there's something
   in the air.
   Hope is stirred, joy's returned,
   faith's conceived:
   it could even be today!

© Sovereign Lifestyle Music

42 Chris Bowater

1. Living on the edge of destiny,
   looking in the face of promises;
   we've never been this way before,
   it could even be today.

2. Breaking through the haze of apathy,
   dawns a new day of expectancy;
   we've never been this way before,
   it could even be today.

3. More than the power of positive thought.
   More than a reason to believe.
   A mirage in the desp'rate eye, oasis of dreams;
   it could even be today!

   Today let this be the day
   when your mighty arm is shown,
   your power by all is known.
   Today, let this be the day,
   we are willing, hearts reach out expecting,
   with one voice declaring: it could even be today!

43 Timothy Dudley-Smith

1. Lord, for the years your love has
   kept and guided,
   urged and inspired us, cheered us
   on our way,
   sought us and saved us, pardoned
   and provided,
   Lord of the years, we bring our
   thanks today.

2. Lord, for that Word, the Word of
   life which fires us,
   speaks to our hearts and sets our
   souls ablaze,
   teaches and trains, rebukes us and
   inspires us,
   Lord of the Word, receive your
   people's praise.

3. Lord, for our land, in this our
   generation,
   spirits oppressed by pleasure, wealth
   and care;
   for young and old, for
   commonwealth and nation,
   Lord of our land, be pleased to hear
   our prayer.

4. Lord, for our world; when we disown and doubt him,
   loveless in strength, and comfortless in pain;
   hungry and helpless, lost indeed without him,
   Lord of the world, we pray that Christ may reign.

5. Lord, for ourselves; in living power remake us,
   self on the cross and Christ upon the throne,
   past put behind us, for the future take us,
   Lord of our lives, to live for Christ alone.

© *Timothy Dudley-Smith*

44 *Timothy Dudley-Smith*

1. Lord of all life and power
   at whose creative word
   in nature's first primeval hour
   our formless being stirred,
   you made the light to shine,
   O shine on us, we pray,
   renew with light and life divine
   your church in this our day.

2. Lord of the fertile earth
   who caused the world to be,
   whose life alone can bring to birth
   the fruits of land and sea,
   teach us to use aright
   and share the gifts you give,
   to tend the earth as in your sight
   that all the world may live.

3. Lord of the cross and grave
   who died and lives again,
   who came in love to seek and save
   and then to rise and reign,
   we share, as once you shared,
   in mortal birth and breath,
   and ours the risen life that dared
   to vanquish sin and death.

4. Lord of the wind and flame,
   the promised Spirit's sign,
   possess our hearts in Jesus' name,
   come down, O Love divine!
   Help us in Christ to grow,
   from sin and self to cease,
   and daily in our lives to show
   your love and joy and peace.

5. Lord of the passing years
   whose changeless purpose stands,
   our lives and loves, our hopes and fears,
   we place within your hands;
   we bring you but your own,
   forgiven, loved and free,
   to follow Christ, and Christ alone,
   through all the days to be.

© *Timothy Dudley-Smith*

45 *Christopher Ellis*

1. Lord of all worlds, we worship and adore you,
   creation sings a galaxy of praise:
   the planets fly, the stars cry out in wonder,
   new life appears, evolving in its ways.

Continued overleaf

2. You forged the sun, the molten
      light of morning;
   you scattered stars, flung jewels of
      the night;
   you are the day which penetrates
      our darkness:
   fill us with hope that we might
      share your light.

3. You summoned land from dark and
      heaving oceans,
   you moulded hills and carved the
      mountains high,
   you are the artist who is still
      creating:
   make us your partners lest the earth
      should die.

4. The glittering shoals flash through
      the rippling water,
   the gliding gull ascends the stream
      of air:
   now leaping thought and
      consecrated action
   become our way of living and of
      prayer.

5. You are the wind that rushes
      through the heavens,
   the breath that gently feeds us from
      our birth:
   we rest in you, our source and goal
      of living,
   we strive for you as stewards of your
      earth.

© 1999 Kevin Mayhew Ltd

46 *Nick Fawcett*

1. Lord, we know that we have failed
      you,
   false and foolish in so much,
   loath to listen to your guidance,
   slow to recognise your touch.
   Though we keep you at a distance,
   by our side, Lord, still remain;
   cleanse our hearts, renew our spirits,
   give us grace to start again.

2. Lord, we know that we have failed
      you
   through the things we do and say,
   though we claim to care for others
   we have thrust their needs away.
   Too concerned with our own comfort
   we have added to their pain;
   teach us to show faith in action,
   give us grace to start again.

3. Lord, we know that we have failed
      you,
   full of doubt when life's been hard;
   suffering has sapped our vision,
   sorrow left our spirits scarred.
   Faced by bitter disappointment
   faith has buckled under strain;
   help us know your hand upon us,
   give us grace to start again.

4. Lord, we know that we have failed
      you,
   too familiar with your word,
   even though you've spoken clearly
   all too often we've not heard.
   Closed to truths which stretch
      horizons
   or which go against the grain –
   teach us, Lord, to stop and listen,
   give us grace to start again.

5. Lord, we know that we have failed you,
   lives too fraught to stop and stare;
   dwelling always on the present –
   what to eat or drink or wear.
   Teach us first to seek your kingdom,
   in our hearts for ever reign;
   send us out, restored, forgiven,
   give us grace to start again.

© *1999 Kevin Mayhew Ltd*

47 *Martin E. Leckebusch*

1. Lord, we thank you for the promise
   seen in ev'ry human birth:
   you have planned each new beginning –
   who could hope for greater worth?
   Hear our prayer for those we cherish;
   claim our children as your own:
   in the fertile ground of childhood
   may eternal seed be sown.

2. Lord, we thank you for the vigour
   burning in the years of youth:
   strength to face tomorrow's challenge,
   zest for life and zeal for truth.
   In the choice of friends and partners,
   when ideas and values form,
   may the message of your kingdom
   be the guide, the goal, the norm.

3. Lord, we thank you for the harvest
   of the settled, middle years:
   times when work and home can prosper,
   when life's richest fruit appears;
   but when illness, stress and hardship
   fill so many days with dread,
   may your love renew the vision
   of a clearer road ahead.

4. Lord, we thank you for the beauty
   of a heart at last mature:
   crowned with peace and rich in wisdom,
   well-respected and secure;
   but to those who face the twilight
   frail, bewildered, lacking friends,
   Lord, confirm your gracious offer:
   perfect life which never ends.

© *1999 Kevin Mayhew Ltd*

48 *P. J. Warren*

May our breath be a song of praise,
may our lives be a sign of grace,
may our words be an anthem raised
   to you.
May our voice speak of victory,
may our hearts strive for unity,
may our deeds serve your majesty
   for you.

All that we have, and all that we are
we lay before your throne.
In your name, and with your power
we pray your will be done.
May our breath be a song of praise
   to you.

© *I.Q. Music Ltd*

49 *Timothy Dudley-Smith*

1. Name of all majesty,
   fathomless mystery,
   King of the ages
   by angels adored;
   power and authority,
   splendour and dignity,
   bow to his mastery –
   Jesus is Lord!

2. Child of our destiny,
   God from eternity,
   love of the Father
   on sinners outpoured;
   see now what God has done
   sending his only Son,
   Christ the beloved One,
   Jesus is Lord!

3. Saviour of Calvary,
   costliest victory,
   darkness defeated
   and Eden restored;
   born as a man to die,
   nailed to a cross on high,
   cold in the grave to lie,
   Jesus is Lord!

4. Source of all sovereignty,
   light, immortality,
   life everlasting
   and heaven assured;
   so with the ransomed, we
   praise him eternally,
   Christ in his majesty,
   Jesus is Lord!

© *Timothy Dudley-Smith*

50 *Paul Wigmore*

1. New light has dawned, the Son of
      God is here,
   a holy light no earthly light
      outshines;
   the light has dawned, the light that
      casts out fear,
   the light that evil dreads and love
      defines.

2. The light of glory shines to angels'
      song,
   the shepherds run to where a baby
      lies;
   a servant of the Lord, who waited
      long,
   acclaims the light to lighten Gentile
      eyes.

3. And priestly men sit listening to a
      boy;
   they see the dawning light within
      his face.
   Such words they hear those Christ-
      child lips employ!
   Amazing words of wisdom, truth
      and grace.

4. O Christ, the light who came to us
      on earth,
   shine through the shadow cast by
      human sin;
   renew the faith you gave at our new
      birth,
   destroy the dark, and let your light
      come in.

© *Paul Wigmore/Jubilate Hymns*

51 *Graham Kendrick*

1. No scenes of stately majesty
   for the King of kings.
   No nights aglow with candle flame
   for the King of love.
   No flags of empire hung in shame
   for Calvary.
   No flowers perfumed the lonely way
   that led him to
   a borrowed tomb for Easter Day.

2. No wreaths upon the ground were laid
   for the King of kings.
   Only a crown of thorns remained
   where he gave his love.
   A message scrawled in irony –
   'King of the Jews' –
   lay trampled where they turned away,
   and no one knew
   that it was the first Easter Day.

3. Yet nature's finest colours blaze
   for the King of kings.
   And stars in jewelled clusters say,
   'Worship heaven's King'.
   Two thousand springtimes more
     have bloomed –
   is that enough?
   Oh, how can I be satisfied
   until he hears
   the whole world sing of Easter love.

4. My prayers shall be a fragrance sweet
   for the King of kings.
   My love the flowers at his feet
   for the King of love.
   My vigil is to watch and pray
   until he comes.
   My highest tribute to obey
   and live to know
   the power of that first Easter Day.

5. I long for scenes of majesty
   for the risen King.
   For nights aglow with candle flame
   for the King of love.
   A nation hushed upon its knees
   at Calvary,
   where all our sins and griefs were nailed
   and hope was born
   of everlasting Easter Day.

© *1997 Ascent Music*

52 *Michael Forster*

1. O God, enthroned in majesty
   and crowned with mortal pain,
   inspired by your amazing love
   we turn to you again;
   for grace and judgement here
     combine
   to meet our deepest need,
   no cheap and easy formula,
   but costly grace, indeed!

2. Confronted by the awesome truth,
   we shrink away in fear:
   all sin is death, the cross proclaims,
   and none stands blameless here.
   Yet through the pain, amazing love
   assures us of your grace,
   and gives us courage to return
   and stand before your face.

3. Now give us grace to stand beneath
   the crosses of the world,
   that all may judge the power of sin,
   yet see your love unfurled.
   Let no more lives be crucified
   by poverty or war,
   but grace and judgement, hand in hand,
   unite to cry, 'no more!'

Continued overleaf

4. Then let the world be freed from
      fear
   to seek love's open way,
   to journey from untimely night
      toward a greater day:
   to justice, hope and liberty,
      the kingdom of your choice,
   when all our praise is gathered up
      in one united voice.

© *1999 Kevin Mayhew Ltd*

5. The Prince of Peace is calling us
      to shun the way of strife:
   he brings us healing through his pain;
      our shattered hope is born again
   through his victorious life.

© *1999 Kevin Mayhew Ltd*

53 *Basil E. Bridge*

1. O God of hope, your prophets
      spoke
   of days when war would cease:
   when, taught to see each person's
      worth,
   and faithful stewards of the earth,
   we all would live in peace.

2. We pray that our divided world
      may hear their words anew:
   then lift for good the curse of war,
   let bread with justice bless the poor,
   and turn in hope to you.

3. Earth's fragile web of life demands
      our reverence and our care,
   lest in our folly, sloth and greed,
   deaf both to you and others' need,
   we lay our plant bare.

4. Earth's rich resources give us power
      to build or to destroy:
   your Spirit urges us to turn
   from selfish, fear-bound ways, and
      learn
   his selfless trust and joy.

54 *Basil E. Bridge*

1. O Lord, our hope in ev'ry
      generation,
   you reigned before the universe
      began:
   we bear your image, we are your
      creation;
   and yet how frail we are, how brief
      life's span.

2. A thousand years like yesterday in
      passing,
   or like the waking memory of our
      dreams,
   like plants that flower at noon but
      die by evening,
   so, Lord, to you our transient glory
      seems.

3. O Holy Lord, forgive our self-
      deceiving;
   our secret sins are clear before your
      face;
   free us to share the joy of those
      believing
   they are restored by your eternal
      grace.

4. Time rushes by: we need your gift
    of wisdom
  to know your will and follow your
    commands;
  your is the power, the glory and the
    kingdom;
  work out your timeless purpose
    through our hands.

© Basil Bridge

55 *Martin E. Leckebusch*

1. Open our eyes to see
   the anguish of the poor –
   indignities untold
   where life is insecure;
   then may our ears discern your call
   to demonstrate your care for all.

2. Open our minds to grasp
   life's grim reality –
   how greed and power prolong
   the curse of poverty;
   and fill our mouths with words to
     speak,
   defending those whose voice is
     weak.

3. Open our hands to give,
   to serve through all our deeds,
   and let our strength be spent
   to meet our neighbours' needs;
   let love, not duty, be our guide:
   Lord, let our hearts be open wide!

© 1999 Kevin Mayhew Ltd

56 *Michael Saward*

1. Overflow with joy and gladness,
   sing, my soul, for freedom gained;
   God has wiped away our sadness
   and the prisoners are unchained.
   Gone the anguish, gone the sorrow,
   gone the manacles of fear;
   faith has triumphed, and tomorrow
   shines with sunlight, bright and clear.

2. Those whose hope is in their Saviour,
   those who trust in Christ their
     Lord,
   now proclaim by their behaviour
   inward peace and true accord.
   Like believers of past ages,
   who for Jesus Christ were bold,
   from such martyrs, saints and sages
   no good thing does God withhold.

3. So, in gratitude, before you,
   God our Father, sun and shield,
   full of praises, we adore you,
   as the powers of darkness yield.
   For this mighty liberation,
   after grief and torment long,
   we rejoice in your salvation:
   hear, O God, our triumph song!

© Michael Saward/Jubilate Hymns

57 *Timothy Dudley-Smith*

1. Praise the Lord of heaven,
   praise him in the height;
   praise him, all his angels,
   praise him, hosts of light.
   Sun and moon together,
   shining stars aflame,
   planets in their courses,
   magnify his name!

Continued overleaf

2. Earth and ocean praise him;
   mountains, hills and trees;
   fire and hail and tempest,
   wind and storm and seas.
   Praise him, fields and forests,
   birds on flashing wings,
   praise him, beasts and cattle,
   all created things.

3. Now by prince and people
   let his praise be told;
   praise him, men and maidens,
   praise him, young and old.
   He, the Lord of glory!
   We, his praise proclaim!
   High above all heavens
   magnify his name!

© *Timothy Dudley-Smith*

58 *Michael Saward*

1. Silently at Christmas
   Jesus came to town,
   homelessness he suffered,
   in a stable born.
   Son of God almighty,
   heir to heaven's crown,
   powerlessness he suffered
   on that morn.

2. Hurriedly at Christmas
   shepherds came to town,
   guilelessness they offered,
   in the humble barn.
   To the Lord almighty
   heir to heaven's crown,
   lowliness they offered
   on that morn.

3. Painfully at Christmas
   people live in town,
   hopelessness they suffer
   hungry and alone.
   Cursing the almighty
   heir to heaven's crown,
   thoughtlessness they suffer
   on this morn.

4. Willingly at Christmas,
   Christians in our town,
   joyfulness they offer,
   carolling the Son,
   and to Christ almighty,
   heir to heaven's crown,
   selflessness they offer
   on this morn.

5. Longingly each Christmas
   Jesus comes to town,
   godlessness he suffers,
   how his heart must burn!
   He is love almighty,
   heir to heaven's crown,
   loneliness he suffers
   on this morn.

© *Michael Saward/Jubilate Hymns*

59 *Michael Saward*

1. Sing glory to God the Father,
   the King of the universe,
     changelessly the same.
   Sing praise to the world's creator
   and magnify his holy name.

   He made all that is round us and all
     that is beyond,
   his hands uphold the planets, to
     him they all respond.

2. Sing glory to God the Saviour,
   the Lord of the galaxies, bearer of our shame.
   Sing praise to the world's redeemer
   and magnify his holy name.

   He suffered grief and torment, for sin he paid the price,
   he rose in glorious triumph, both priest and sacrifice.

3. Sing glory to God the Spirit,
   the power of the elements, setting hearts aflame.
   Sing praise to the world's life-giver
   and magnify his holy name.

   His gifts to all are given, his fruit transforms our hearts,
   his fellowship enriches, a grace which he imparts.

4. Sing glory, the whole creation!
   Give thanks to the Trinity, heaven's love proclaim.
   Sing praise to our God, almighty,
   and magnify his holy name.

© Michael Saward/Jubilate Hymns

60 *Michael Forster*

Stars: shine!
Bells: chime!
Angels: tell us that it's really true.
God is in his world, and his world is new.

1. Come, let us meet at the manger,
   learn from the child who is born.
   New life begins at the manger,
   life that's as fresh as the dawn.

2. Families meet at the manger,
   learn from the child who is Word.
   New life begins at the manger,
   life where all voices are heard.

3. Governments meet at the manger,
   learn from the child who is Lord.
   New life begins at the manger,
   life that is free from the sword.

4. Come, let us meet at the manger,
   learn from the child who is Love.
   New life begins at the manger,
   life as a gift from above.

© 1999 Kevin Mayhew Ltd

61 *Verses 1 and 3 Margaret Rizza; verse 2 unknown*

1. Take my hands, Lord, to share in your labours,
   take my eyes, Lord, to see your needs,
   let me hear the voice of lonely people,
   let my love, Lord, bring riches to the poor.

2. Give me someone to feed when I'm hungry,
   when I'm thirsty, give water for their thirst.
   When I stand in need of tenderness,
   give me someone to hold who longs for love.

3. Keep my heart ever open to others,
   may my time, Lord, be spent with those in need;
   may I tend to those who need your care.
   Take my life, Lord, and make me truly yours.

© 1999 Kevin Mayhew Ltd

62 *Andrew Gant*

1. Take my heart, Lord God of my
      creation,
   take my eyes, Lord God who makes
      me see,
   take my mind, Lord God who
      makes me worship;
   to be your servant, Lord; take me.

2. Take my strength, Lord God of
      dedication,
   take my anger, Lord who calmed
      the sea,
   take my love, Lord God who came
      to love me;
   to be your stronghold, Lord; take me.

3. Take my thoughts, Lord God of
      inspiration,
   take my hands, take my humanity,
   take my friends, Lord God who
      shared your friendship;
   for your compassion, Lord; take me.

4. Take my path, Lord God of
      inspiration,
   take my sins, Lord God who sets
      me free,
   take my soul, Lord God who knows
      my weakness;
   to be your pilgrim, Lord; take me.

5. Take my life, Lord God of
      resurrection,
   take my all, Lord God who holds
      the key,
   take my heart, Lord God whose
      heart was broken;
   for your disciple, Lord; take me.

© 1999 Kevin Mayhew Ltd

63 *Michael Saward*

1. Thanks be to God
   for his most holy Son.
   Our hearts we lift
   in adoration now.

2. Thanks be to God
   for all the Spirit's power.
   Our hearts we lift
   in liberation now.

3. Thanks be to God
   for giving us new birth.
   Our hearts we lift
   in consecration now.

4. Thanks be to God
   for eucharistic food.
   Our hearts we lift
   in exultation now.

5. Thanks be to God
   for hope of heaven's joy.
   Our hearts we lift
   in expectation now.

6. Thanks be to God,
   blessed Trinity above.
   Our hearts we lift
   in veneration now.

© Michael Saward/Jubilate Hymns

64 *Michael Saward*

1. The kingdom of the living God
   has come, as Christ proclaimed;
   for he, the King, has, on his throne
   the human heart reclaimed,
   when, crowned with thorns, upon
      the cross,
   his kingship has been named.

2. In action and in parable
that kingdom has been taught.
Its character, transforming lives,
is by disciples sought;
for Jesus, with the blood he shed,
has our salvation bought.

3. This King has our allegiance won,
our lives to him are bound,
he calls us as his royal priests
to treat as holy ground
the whole wide world for which he died
and rose, and now is crowned.

4. And yet we pray, 'Your kingdom come',
that holy city bright,
for he who came a peasant babe
shall come in radiant light
to bring that kingdom here to earth
and reign in glorious might.

© Michael Saward/Jubilate Hymns

65 *June L. Baker*

1. The road through life, the road is long and hard,
O Lord, my feet are weary and sore;
the going's rough and things are getting tough,
but, Lord, I know you've gone before.

Roads, Lord, roads, Lord,
how hard my road can be,
take me by the hand
and walk this road with me.

2. The map of life is not too clear to read,
and I get lost on many a day;
the going's rough and things are getting tough,
but, Lord, I know you know the way.

3. Sometimes ahead the road is black as night
and ev'ry step is full of fear;
the going's rough and things are getting tough,
but, Lord, I know that you are here.

© 1999 Kevin Mayhew Ltd

66 *Michael Forster*

1. The universe was waiting
in dark, chaotic night,
until the word was spoken:
'Let there be glorious light!'
From darkness and from chaos
were light and order born;
the God of new beginnings
rejoiced to see their dawn.

2. And as in that beginning,
in every age the same,
creation's Re-creator
is keeping hope aflame.
From Eden to the desert,
the manger to the tomb,
each fall becomes a rising,
and every grave a womb.

Continued overleaf

3. Wherever people languish
   in darkness or despair,
   the God of new beginnings
   is pierced, and rises there.
   We join with him, to listen,
   to care, and to protest,
   to see the mighty humbled
   and all the humble blessed.

4. We join with our Creator
   to keep the vision bright:
   in places of oppression
   we call for freedom's light:
   a glorious new beginning,
   a universe at peace,
   where justice flows like fountains
   and praises never cease.

© 1999 Kevin Mayhew Ltd

67 *Dave Bilbrough*

1. This is the time of celebration.
   This is the season of great joy.
   All over the world God's Spirit is
      moving.
   Now is the time to rejoice!

2. Two thousand years since his
      coming
   Jesus still calls us to share his love.
   With voices that speak for truth
      and justice,
   offering hope to everyone.

   Come and worship him,
   come and worship him,
   come and worship him:
   Jesus the Lord.
   (Repeat)

Break free from all your
   distractions;
join your hearts in one accord;
and take the message of the
   kingdom
to the lost and lonely, to the rich
   and poor.

3. Spread the Good News of God's
      compassion.
   Lift up your eyes with faith and
      prayer.
   The fields are now ready for the
      harvest.
   Go tell the people everywhere.

© 1999 Kingsway's Thankyou Music

68 *Graham Kendrick*

1. Through days of rage and wonder
   we pursue the end of time,
   to seize the day eternal,
   the reign of love divine.

2. Fixing our eyes on Jesus,
   we will press on day by day;
   this world's vain passing pleasures
   are not our destiny.
   Our ancient rites of passage
   still are the bread and wine:
   our hope a cross that towers
   over the wrecks of time.

3. Through days of rage and wonder,
   by the awesome power of prayer
   God will shake every nation,
   secrets will be laid bare.
   And if his light increasing
   casts deeper shadows here,
   safe in his holy presence,
   love will cast out our fear.

4. Through days of rage and wonder
you will give us strength to stand
and seek a heavenly city
not built by human hands.
Now is the only moment
within our power to change:
to give back in obedience
while life and breath remain.

© 1999 Make Way Music

69 *Brian Hoare*

1. Two thousand years since Bethlehem
first welcomed Jesus' birth:
the startling truth began to dawn
that God had come to earth.
And as he grew and lived and taught
a different way unfurled:
a way of joy and love and peace,
a new start for the world!

2. Two thousand years since Galilee
where Jesus preached and healed;
in words of truth and works of power
God's kingdom was revealed.
As young and old and rich and poor
responded to his call,
they found what we may find today:
a new start for us all!

3. Two thousand years since Calvary,
the hill where Jesus died;
the Lamb of God, the sinless one,
for me was crucified.
But soon he rose up from the grave
to reign in victory;
goods news I scarcely can believe:
a new start won for me!

4. Two thousand years since Pentecost:
the Holy Spirit came
in sound of mighty, rushing wind
and tongues of living flame;
a gift to all who will believe
and live the Jesus way;
the power of God we may receive,
a new start from today!

5. Two thousand years of Christian faith
have changed our history,
for Jesus is the Lord of time
and of eternity.
For all who seek a better way,
than failure, sin and pain,
still Jesus Christ makes all things new:
a chance to start again!

© Brian Hoare/Jubilate Hymns

70 *Nick Fawcett*

1. Warm as the sun,
fresh as the breeze,
fair as a flower,
tall as the trees,
clear as the dew,
pure as the dove,
so unto me,
Lord, is your love.

2. Lovely as dawn,
welcome as light,
peaceful as dusk,
restful as night,
high as the clouds,
deep as the sea,
so is your love,
Lord, unto me.

Continued overleaf

3. Swift as a stream,
   free as a bird,
   firm as a rock,
   sure as your word,
   bright as the stars,
   shining above,
   so unto me,
   Lord, is your love.

4. Finer than silk,
   richer than money,
   precious as gold,
   sweeter than honey,
   priceless as jewels,
   dear as can be,
   so is your love,
   Lord, unto me.

5. Bursting with joy,
   leaping with praise,
   glowing with thanks,
   heart set ablaze;
   bringing my life,
   all that I do,
   such is my love,
   Jesus, for you.

© 1999 Kevin Mayhew Ltd

71 Randle Manwaring

1. We shall see him in the morning
   when the mists of life have cleared,
   with his arms outstretched to greet us
   from a journey we had feared.

2. *Men*
   Those who toiled all night and struggled
   till the earthly fight was won
   will awaken to the music
   of his welcoming 'Well done!'

3. *Women*
   We shall recognise the Master
   with his wounded hands and side
   as we worship him, the glorious,
   the ascended Crucified.

4. Though the shore now seems so distant
   we await the morning light
   and the breakfast celebration
   when our faith gives way to sight.

© 1999 Kevin Mayhew Ltd

72 Christopher Ellis

1. What shall we bring to give honour to God:
   worship and sacrifice, praying and song?
   This is all nothing unless we can bring
   justice and mercy to honour our King.

   Walk with our God, humbly each day.
   Help us to do all that we say.
   Justice and mercy should crown all we bring –
   this is the worship we offer our King.

2. Save us, O Lord, from the hypocrite's prayer:
   bringing you praise while our deeds are unfair.
   Help us to honour all people on earth:
   each one is precious, of infinite worth.

3. Save us, O Lord, from excuse and neglect,
   show us the world as you see it today.
   Kindle within us a passion for good;
   give us the strength to do all that we should.

© *1999 Kevin Mayhew Ltd*

Index of Authors

Anderson, Mike	15	Holloway, Jean	22
Aspinwall, John	6	Idle, Christopher	20
Baker, Geoff	29	Kendrick, Graham	18, 51, 68
Baker, June L.	65	Leckebusch, Martin E.	9, 12, 31, 39, 47, 55
Bartleet, David	33	Manwaring, Randle	71
Bell, John L.	17	Maule, Graham	17
Berry, Jan	13, 41	Mowbray, David	40
Bilbrough, Dave	67	Quinn, James	32
Bowater, Chris	14, 42	Rizza, Margaret	34, 61
Bridge, Basil E.	7, 26, 35, 53, 54	Saward, Michael	56, 58, 59, 63, 64
Cosnett, Elizabeth	21	Taylor, Ian	14
Dobson, Marjorie	4, 10	Trow, Peter	24
Dudley-Smith, Timothy	25, 28, 43, 44, 49, 57	Wakeman, Rick	38
Ellis, Christopher	1, 2, 23, 45, 72,	Walker, Christopher	27
Fawcett, Nick	30, 36, 46, 70,	Warren, P. J.	48
Forster, Michael	11, 19, 37, 52, 60, 66	Wigmore, Paul	50
Gant, Andrew	62	Williams, Catherine	16
Hoare, Brian	3, 5, 8, 69		

Thematic Index

The hymns and songs in this collection were written to focus particularly on the themes chosen for the Millennium. These themes are:

A New Start for the World's Poor
A New Start at Home
A New Start with God

A New Start for the World's Poor

Beyond the fringes of the church	3
Bright, bright, the shining of Christ's saving way	6
Christ brings the kingdom	9
Come and join the great uprising	11
Come, wounded Healer	12
Creating God, we bring our song of praise	13
Every fiftieth year	17
First light	18
God of every changing season	21
Gracious God, in adoration	26
Great is the power we proclaim	27
Here on the threshold of a new beginning	28
I hear somebody calling	30
In an age of twisted values	31
Jesus, in your life we see you	35
Jesus, the broken bread	36
Join the glorious celebration	37
Light a candle for thanksgiving!	40
Lord, for the years	43
Lord, we know that we have failed you	46
O God, enthroned in majesty	52
O God of hope	53
Open our eyes	55
Silently at Christmas	58
Stars: shine!	60
Take my hands, Lord	61
The universe was waiting	66
This is the time of celebration	67
What shall we bring	72

A New Start at Home

Birth brings a promise	4
God made a boomerang	19
God of the passing centuries	24
In an age of twisted values	31
Light a candle for thanksgiving!	40
Lord, we thank you for the promise	47
Stars: shine!	60

A New Start with God

Almighty God, we come to make confession	1
At the heart of all things	2
Beyond the fringes of the church	3
Birth brings a promise	4
Blessing and honour	5
Bright, bright, the shining of Christ's saving way	6
But when the time had fully come	7
Celebrate the faith together	8
Christ brings the kingdom	9
Christian people, sing together	10
Come and join the great uprising	11
Come, wounded Healer	12
Creating God, we bring our song of praise	13
Creation is awaiting	14
Dance in your Spirit	15
Deep within the shadow of your wings	16
Every fiftieth year	17
First light	18
God made a boomerang	19
God of all human history	20
God of every changing season	21
God of love	22
God of mission, still you send us	23
God of the passing centuries	24
God whose love is everywhere	25
Gracious God, in adoration	26
Great is the power we proclaim	27
Here on the threshold of a new beginning	28
If my people, who are called by my name	29
I hear somebody calling	30
In an age of twisted values	31
In the silence of the Godhead	32
I saw the wind in the sky	33
Jesus, in the new dawn	34
Jesus, in your life we see you	35
Jesus, the broken bread	36
Join the glorious celebration	37
Just one world	38
Let us rejoice	39
Light a candle for thanksgiving!	40
Living God, your word has called us	41
Living on the edge of destiny	42
Lord, for the years	43
Lord of all life and power	44
Lord of all worlds	45
Lord, we know that we have failed you	46
Lord, we thank you for the promise	47
May our breath be a song of praise	48
Name of all majesty	49
New light has dawned	50
No scenes of stately majesty	51
O God, enthroned in majesty	52
O Lord, our hope in every generation	54
Overflow with joy and gladness	56
Praise the Lord of heaven	57
Silently at Christmas	58
Sing glory to God the Father	59
Stars: shine!	60
Take my heart	62
Thanks be to God	63
The kingdom of the living God	64
The road through life	65
The universe was waiting	66
This is the time of celebration	67
Through days of rage and wonder	68
Two thousand years since Bethlehem	69
Warm as the sun	70
We shall see him in the morning	71
What shall we bring	72

Scriptural Index

GENESIS
1:1 — 25
1:1-2 — 59
1:1-5 — 44, 66
1:1-28 — 45
1:3-25 — 57
1:16 — 25
1:27 — 26, 32
1:28 — 44
1:31 — 26
2:7 — 26
4:10 — 30
8:22 — 25

LEVITICUS
25:2 — 17
25:8-10 — 17
25:10 — 40
25:28 — 17

DEUTERONOMY
31:8 — 47

JOSHUA
3:4 — 42
14:10-12 — 47

1 SAMUEL
7:12 — 28

2 CHRONICLES
7:14 — 31
7:14-15 — 29

JOB
38:7 — 34

PSALMS
2:7 — 4, 32
19:1-4 — 26, 33, 45, 51
22:1 — 35
23:4 — 65
25:1-3 — 39
27:14 — 16
32:1-5 — 1, 46
33:12 — 31, 43
34:8 — 70
37:25 — 47
46:1-11 — 39
46:9-11 — 53
48:12-13 — 40, 47
51:1-2 — 30
51:1-4 — 46
51:1-12 — 1
63:7 — 16
71:18 — 40, 47
78:4 — 40, 47
84:11 — 56
90:1-2 — 20, 24, 43, 44, 47
90:1-17 — 54
91:4 — 16
93:3-4 — 57
95:1-2 — 10
95:1-6 — 59
95:1-7 — 26
95:7-8 — 42
96:11-13 — 57
97:1 — 28
98:4-9 — 17
100:1-3 — 13
100:1-5 — 43, 56
103:11 — 39, 70
103:20-22 — 57
104:1-30 — 57
104:30 — 44
107:1-43 — 40
110:1 — 14
133:1 — 10, 27, 41
139:14-16 — 47
147:5 — 27
149:3 — 15

PROVERBS
3:5-6 — 34, 39, 47, 65
8:22-30 — 32
13:34 — 31
14:34 — 43

SONG OF SOLOMON
1:2-3 — 70
2:11 — 42
2:11-12 — 18
4:10-11 — 70

ISAIAH
1:18-19 — 29
2:3-5 — 53
6:8 — 3
9:2-7 — 53
11:1-5 — 18
35:1 — 14
40:31 — 16
49:2 — 16
49:16 — 35
53:3-5 — 12
53:4 — 13, 35
53:4-5 — 53
53:4-6 — 24
55:12 — 14
56:1 — 30
58:6-7 — 17, 30, 37, 55, 72
59:15-17 — 30
61:1-2 — 26, 28, 40
61:1-3 — 6, 9, 37, 43, 56
61:1-4 — 17, 30
64:1 — 17, 42
66:17 — 17

JOEL
2:28 — 67

AMOS
5:23-24 — 72
5:24 — 66

MICAH
4:2-4 — 53
6:6-8 — 72
6:8 — 30

HAGGAI
2:6 — 68
2:21 — 68

ZECHARIAH
8:4-5 — 31, 47

MALACHI
4:2 — 18

MATTHEW
4:17 — 9, 64
5:5 — 30, 55
5:6 — 36
5:7 — 30, 55
5:9 — 30
5:14-16 — 3, 28, 50
6:10 — 3, 9, 26, 28, 36, 43, 48, 51, 52, 64, 66
6:12 — 1, 29, 34, 46
6:24 — 21, 31
6:31-33 — 43
6:33 — 21, 36, 46, 47
7:24 — 6
8:16-17 — 64
9:36 — 35

9:37	67
11:28-30	12, 17
13:1-52	64
13:20-22	46
16:16	7
18:21-35	1
18:35	34
24:14	20, 37, 67
24:35	22
25:1-13	14
25:34-40	61
25:40	55, 66
26:14-16	7
26:41	51
26:47-50	7
26:56	7
27:32-61	51
27:35	7
27:37	64
28:1-10	7
28:6	32
28:18-20	3, 8, 20, 23, 37, 67
28:20	47

MARK

1:15	9
3:5	7
6:1-6	7
10:43-45	27
10:45	12, 22, 25, 26, 69
11:22-24	42
11:25	34
14:38	51
14:43-46	7
14:50	7
15:21-47	51
15:24	7
15:26	64
16:1-8	7
16:6	32

LUKE

1:52	66
2:4	69
2:4-7	60
2:4-20	58
2:13-16	50
2:25-35	50
2:46-50	50
4:18-19	6, 9, 11, 17, 26, 28, 30, 35, 37, 40, 43, 56, 69
10:1	23
10:25-37	3
10:27	26, 27, 30, 55, 62
15:11-24	46
15:18-24	9
17:21	64
19:10	44

22:3-6	7
22:14-30	36
22:47-48	7
23:26-56	51
23:33	7
23:38	64
24:1-8	7
24:6	32

JOHN

1:1	43
1:1-2	60
1:1-5	44
1:1-18	32
1:12-14	27
1:14	4, 21, 69
1:29	69
3:3	4, 18, 34, 63
3:8	22, 45
3:16	2, 25, 30, 32, 35, 37, 38, 44, 49, 59, 70
4:24	36
4:35	67
6:35	36, 63
6:53-56	63
6:53-57	36
8:12	6, 18, 25, 28, 34, 40, 45, 50
10:10	11, 38
10:16	3
10:27-29	47
12:6	7
12:23-26	27
12:24	32
13:2	7
13:27-30	7
13:34-35	2, 19, 24, 27, 30, 36, 41
14:1	39
14:6	6, 15, 31, 34, 38
14:27	24, 27, 34, 39
15:1-8	16
15:12	2, 19, 24, 41, 60
15:15	23
16:21-22	4
16:24	24, 34
17:20-21	10, 27
17:21	23
17:22-23	33
18:2-8	7
19:16-42	51
19:18	7
20:1-9	7
20:21	36
20:22	5
20:26-28	12
20:27	35
20:28	8
21:4-13	71

ACTS

1:3	32
1:8	5, 8
1:10-11	71
2:1-4	5, 44, 69
2:3	25
2:17	23
2:22-24	7
2:24	18, 66
2:27	18
2:39	3
10:38	69

ROMANS

1:4	8
1:16	8
1:20	26, 33, 51
1:21-23	31
2:16	68
4:17	26
4:18	42
5:2	20
5:5	39, 70
6:6-11	38
8:10-11	38
8:17	28
8:17-23	21
8:18-23	6
8:18-27	52
8:19-21	14
8:19-22	30
8:22-23	4
8:29	9, 20, 29
12:1-2	35, 43, 48, 62, 68
12:11	70
12:11-12	36
14:17	9, 13, 18
15:13	22, 23, 37

1 CORINTHIANS

1:18-31	12
1:20	24
1:25	21, 22
1:30	6
11:26	27, 68
12:4-11	59
12:4-27	10
12:27	41
14:12	27
15:3-4	44, 59, 69
15:53-57	18
15:55-57	11

2 CORINTHIANS

1:3-11	52
3:17	15, 63
3:18	6, 10
4:6	6

2 CORINTHIANS (continued)
4:6-12	52
5:7	69
5:14	27
5:17	18
5:17-21	52
6:2	20, 42
8:9	12, 49
8:19	52
9:15	63
13:14	22, 59

GALATIANS
2:20	43
3:26-28	21
3:28	23, 30, 31, 37, 41
4:4	22
4:4-5	7
5:22-23	15, 44, 59
6:14	68

EPHESIANS
1:3-10	37
2:6	11, 44
2:8	24, 28
2:14-18	30, 31
2:21-22	28
3:14	31
4:3-6	10, 22, 41
4:13	20
4:14	44
5:1-2	44
5:8-14	50
5:13-14	25
5:25	31, 40, 47
5:25-27	14
5:33	40, 47
5:35	31
6:1-4	31, 40
6:10	27
6:13	68

PHILIPPIANS
1:21	47
2:5-11	32, 49, 69
2:6-11	5

2:9-11	8, 14, 67
2:11	60
3:10-14	42, 44
3:13-14	21, 68
3:20	21
4:4	70

COLOSSIANS
1:15	18
1:15-20	32
1:17	25
1:27	43
2:13-15	11
2:15	22
3:1-3	11
3:1-4	15
3:12-17	10

1 THESSALONIANS
4:13-18	71

1 TIMOTHY
1:17	49
3:16	49
6:10	21, 31

2 TIMOTHY
1:10	36, 49
3:14-17	43
3:16-17	28
4:7-8	47

HEBREWS
1:1-3	32
2:14-15	11
2:15	18
11:1	28
11:10	68
12:2	68
12:24	30
12:26-29	68

JAMES
1:22-25	31
1:27	55
2:14-26	46

1 PETER
1:3	63
1:8	70
2:7	70
2:24	35

2 PETER
1:19	45
3:13	13, 66

1 JOHN
1:1-4	21
1:5-10	46
1:8-10	1
1:9	24, 28, 29, 30, 31, 33
2:1-2	1, 13, 46
2:2	21, 30, 59, 64
3:1	22, 34
3:8	11, 21
4:7-8	19
4:7-12	2, 33
4:7-14	60
4:10	12, 25, 28
4:10-11	70
4:18	15, 21, 24, 26, 50, 52, 56, 68
4:19	19

REVELATION
1:17-18	18
1:18	36
4:11	5, 13
5:6	12
5:9	8, 10, 30, 37
5:12	8
5:13	5
19:16	36
21:1	11, 13, 17, 18
21:2	14, 64
21:4	17
21:5	6, 13, 18, 24, 37, 69

Index of First Lines and Titles

This index gives the first line of each hymn. If a hymn is known by an alternative title, this is also given, but indented and in italics.

A

Almighty God, we come to make confession	1
At the heart of all things	2

B

Beyond the fringes of the church	3
Birth brings a promise	4
Blessing and honour	5
Bright, bright, the shining of Christ's saving way	6
But when the time had fully come	7

C

Celebrate the faith together	8
Christ brings the kingdom	9
Christian people, sing together	10
Christingle Hymn	25
Come and join the great uprising	11
Come, wounded Healer	12
Creating God, we bring our song of praise	13
Creation is awaiting	14

D

Dance in your Spirit	15
Deep within the shadow of your wings	16

E

Every fiftieth year	17

F

First light	18
From eternity to eternity	32

G

God made a boomerang	19
God of all human history	20
God of every changing season	21
God of love	22
God of mission, still you send us	23
God of the passing centuries	24
God whose love is everywhere	25
Gracious God, in adoration	26
Great is the power we proclaim	27

H

Heal our nation	31
Here on the threshold of a new beginning	28
Hope of glory	42

I

If my people, who are called by my name	29
I hear somebody calling	30
In an age of twisted values	31
In the silence of the Godhead	32
I saw the wind in the sky	33

J

Jesus, in the new dawn	34
Jesus, in your life we see you	35
Jesus, the broken bread	36
Join the glorious celebration	37
Jubilee	17
Just one world	38

L

Let us rejoice	39
Light a candle for thanksgiving!	40
Living God, your word has called us	41
Living on the edge of destiny	42
Lord, for the years	43
Lord of all life and power	44
Lord of all worlds	45
Lord, we know that we have failed you	46
Lord, we thank you for the promise	47

M

May our breath be a song of praise	48

N

Name of all majesty	49
New light has dawned	50
No scenes of stately majesty	51

O

O God, enthroned in majesty	52
O God of hope	53
O Lord, our hope in every generation	54
Open our eyes	55
Overflow with joy and gladness	56

P

Praise the Lord of heaven	57

S

Silently at Christmas	58
Sing glory to God the Father	59
Stars: shine!	60

T

Take my hands, Lord	61
Take my heart	62
Take my life	61
Thanks be to God	63
The kingdom of the living God	64
The road through life	65
The universe was waiting	66
This is the time of celebration	67
Through days of rage and wonder	68
Today, let this be the day	41
Two thousand years since Bethlehem	69

W

Warm as the sun	70
We shall see him in the morning	71
What shall we bring	72

Acknowledgements

The publishers wish to express their gratitude to the following for permission to include copyright material in this publication. Details of copyright owners are given underneath each individual hymn.

Ascent Music, PO Box 263, Croydon, CR9 5AP. International copyright secured. All rights reserved.

The Rt Revd David Bartleet, 21 Lee Road, Aldeburgh, Suffolk, IP15 5EY.

The Revd Basil Bridge, 124 Linacre Avenue, Sprowston, Norwich, NR7 8JS.

Geoffrey Chapman (an imprint of Cassell plc), 125 Strand, London, WC2R 0BB.

Bishop Timothy Dudley-Smith, 9 Ashlands, Ford, Salisbury, Wiltshire, SP4 6DY.

Wild Goose Resource Group, Iona Community, Pearce Institute, 840 Govan Road, Glasgow, G51 3UU.

IQ Music Ltd, Commercial House, 52 Perrymount Road, Haywards Heath, W. Sussex, RH16 3DT.

Jubilate Hymns, 4 Thorne Park Road, Chelston, Torquay, TQ2 6RX.

Kingsway's Thankyou Music, PO Box 75, Eastbourne, E. Sussex, BN23 6NW.

Make Way Music, PO Box 263, Croydon, CR9 5AP. International copyright secured. All rights reserved.

OCP Publications, 5536 NE Hassalo, Portland, OR 97213, USA. All rights reserved.

Sovereign Music UK, PO Box 356, Leighton Buzzard, Beds., LU7 8WP.

Sovereign Lifestyle Music Ltd, PO Box 356, Leighton Buzzard, Beds., LU7 8WP.

Stainer & Bell Ltd, PO Box 110, Victoria House, 23 Gruneisen Road, Finchley, London, N3 1DZ.

Tuesday Music (UK) Ltd, 45 Mount Ash Road, London, SE26 6LY. All rights reserved.

Catherine Williams, St Margaret's Cottage, St Margaret's Street, Rochester, ME1 1SX.

All other material in this book is the copyright of Kevin Mayhew Ltd. Every effort has been made to trace the owners of copyright material and we hope that no copyright has been infringed. Pardon is sought and apology made if the contrary be the case, and a correction will be made in any reprint of this book.